Lupita Romo

Cute Animals

Coloring Book
For children

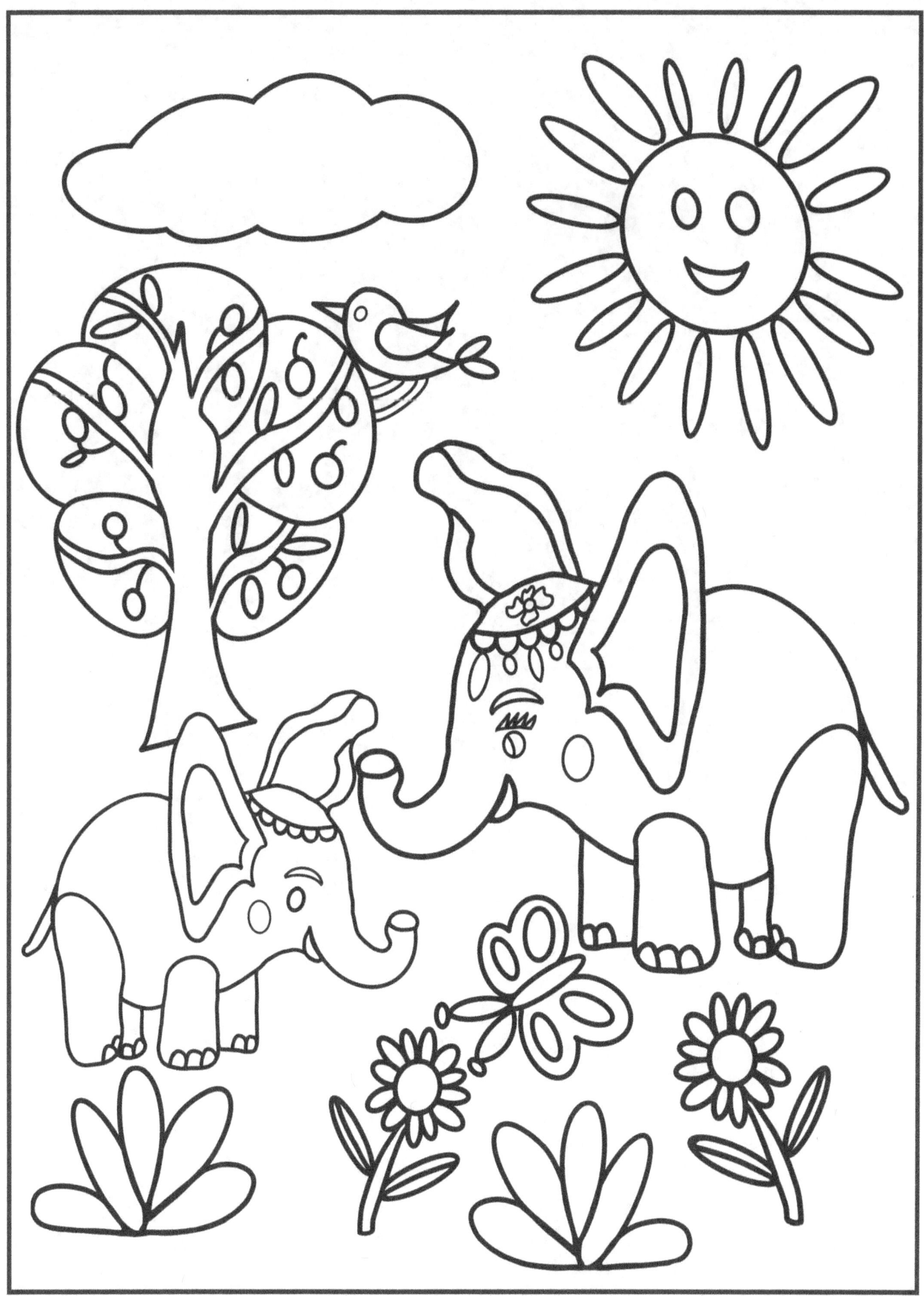

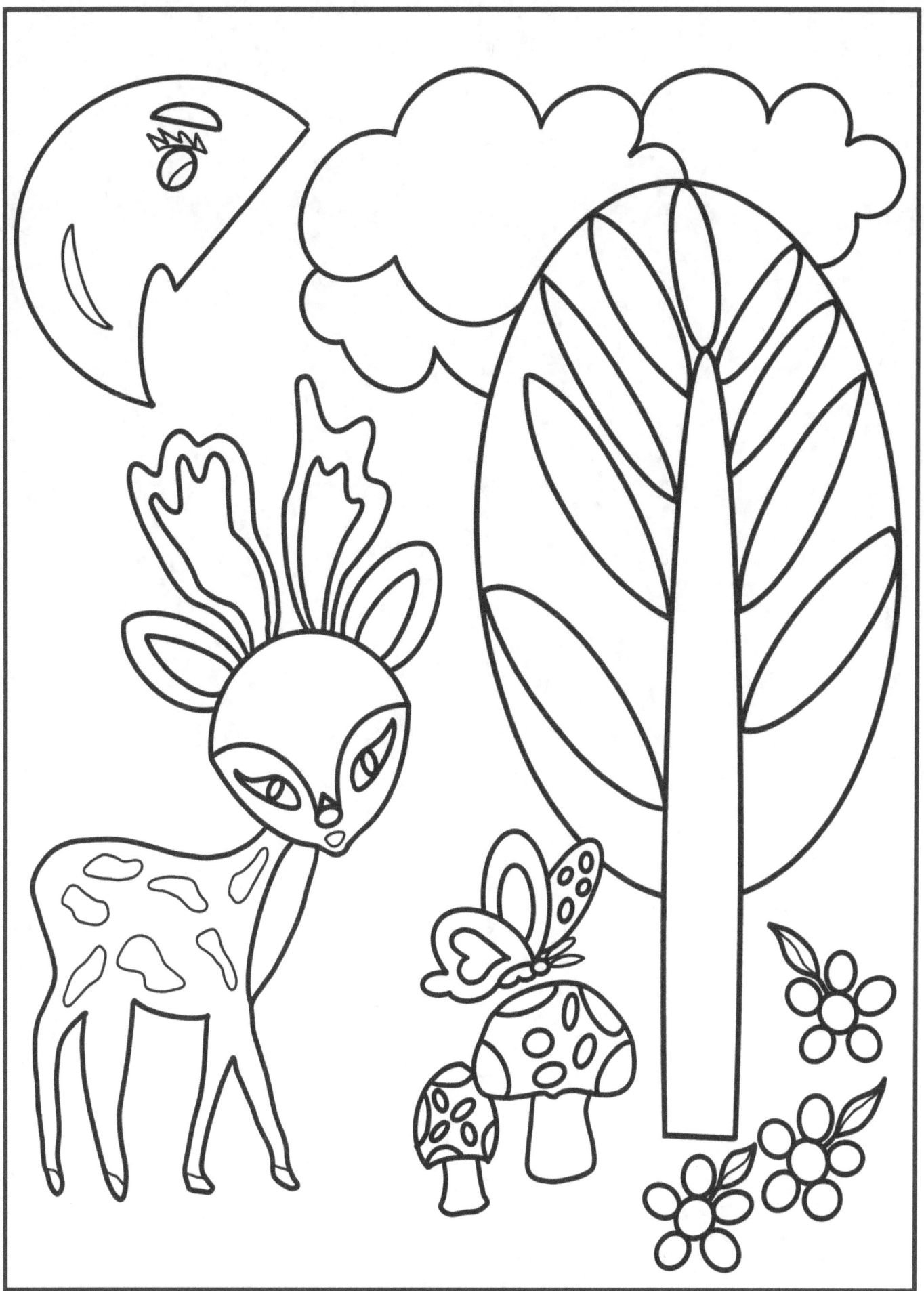

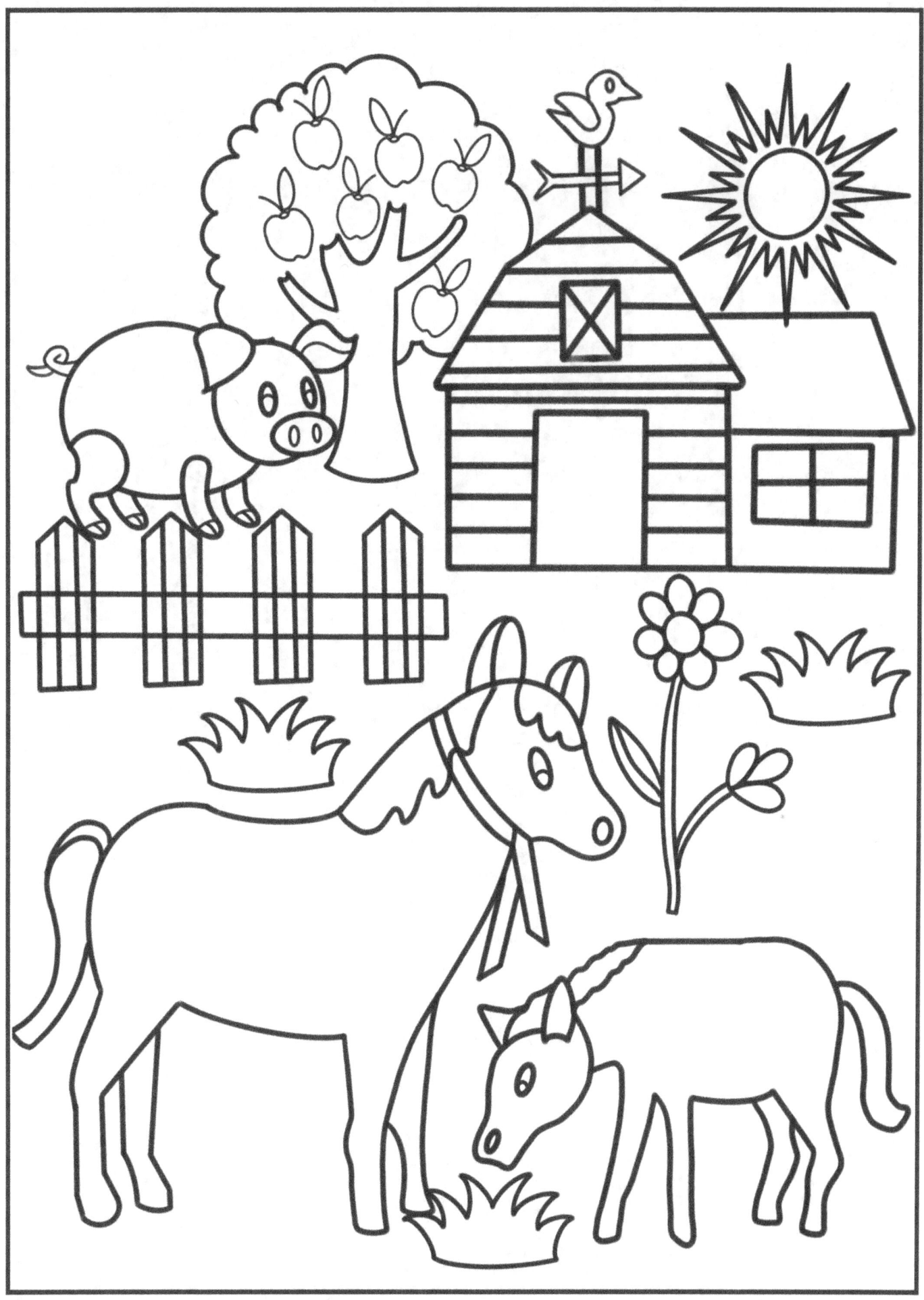

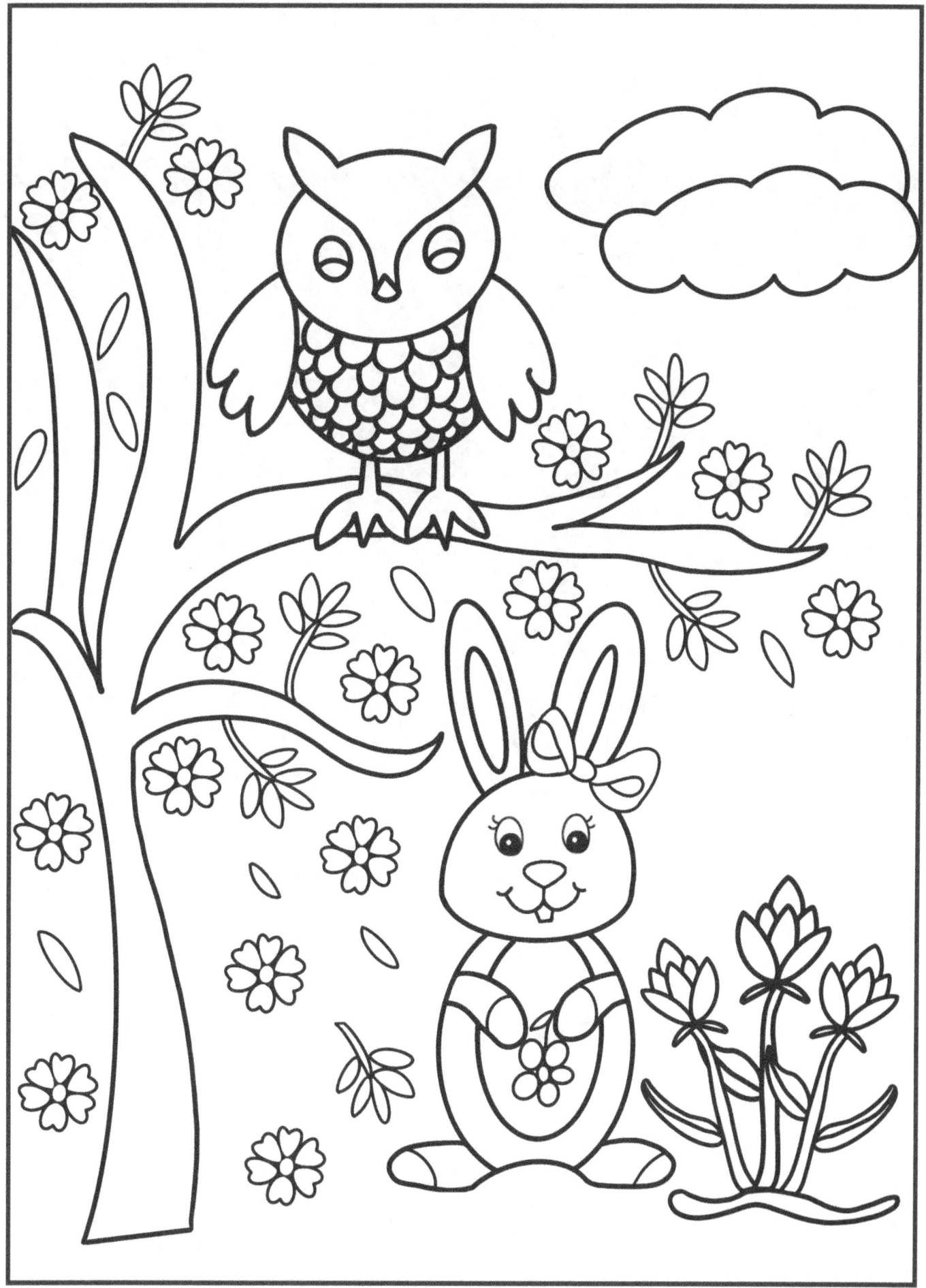

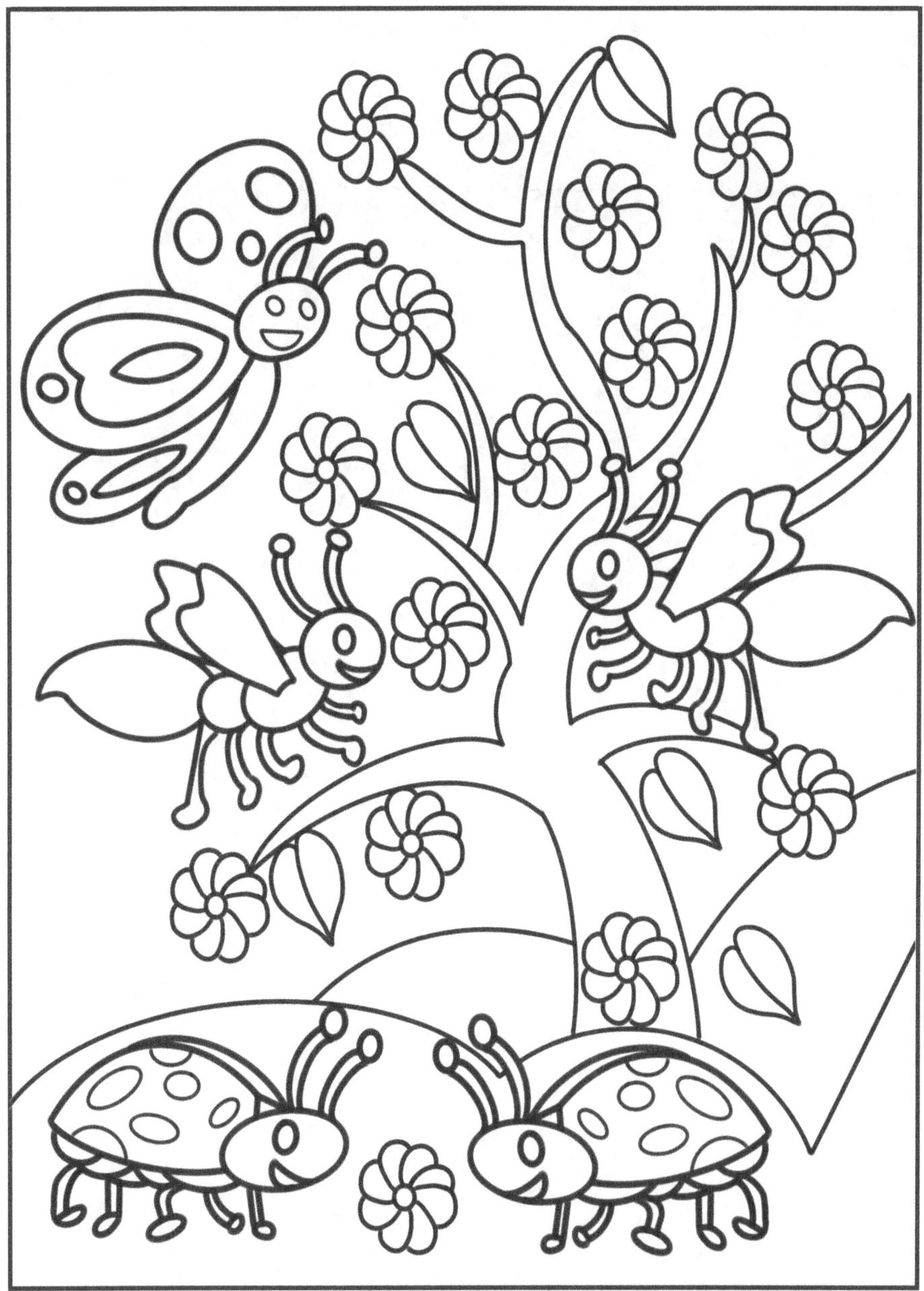

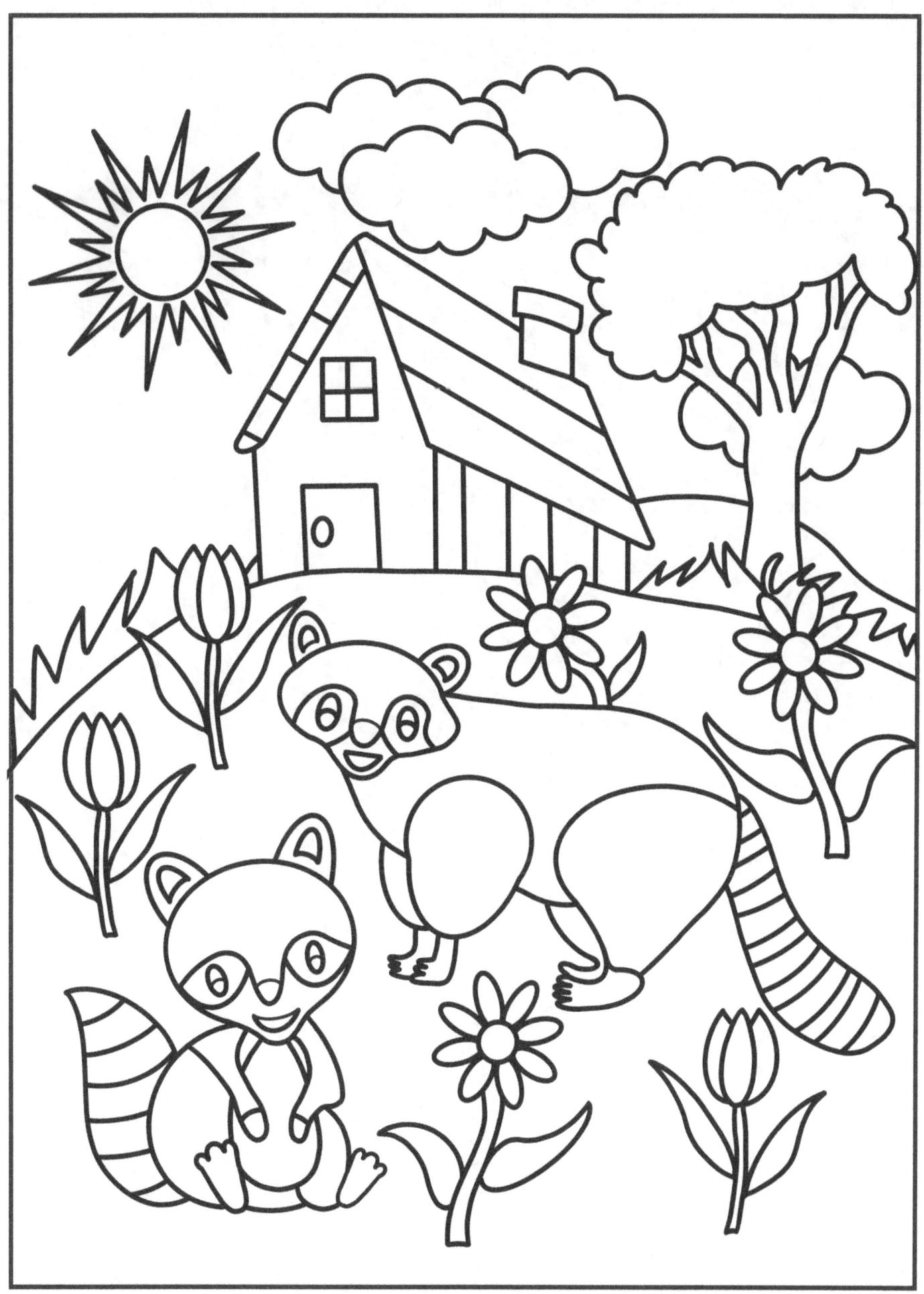

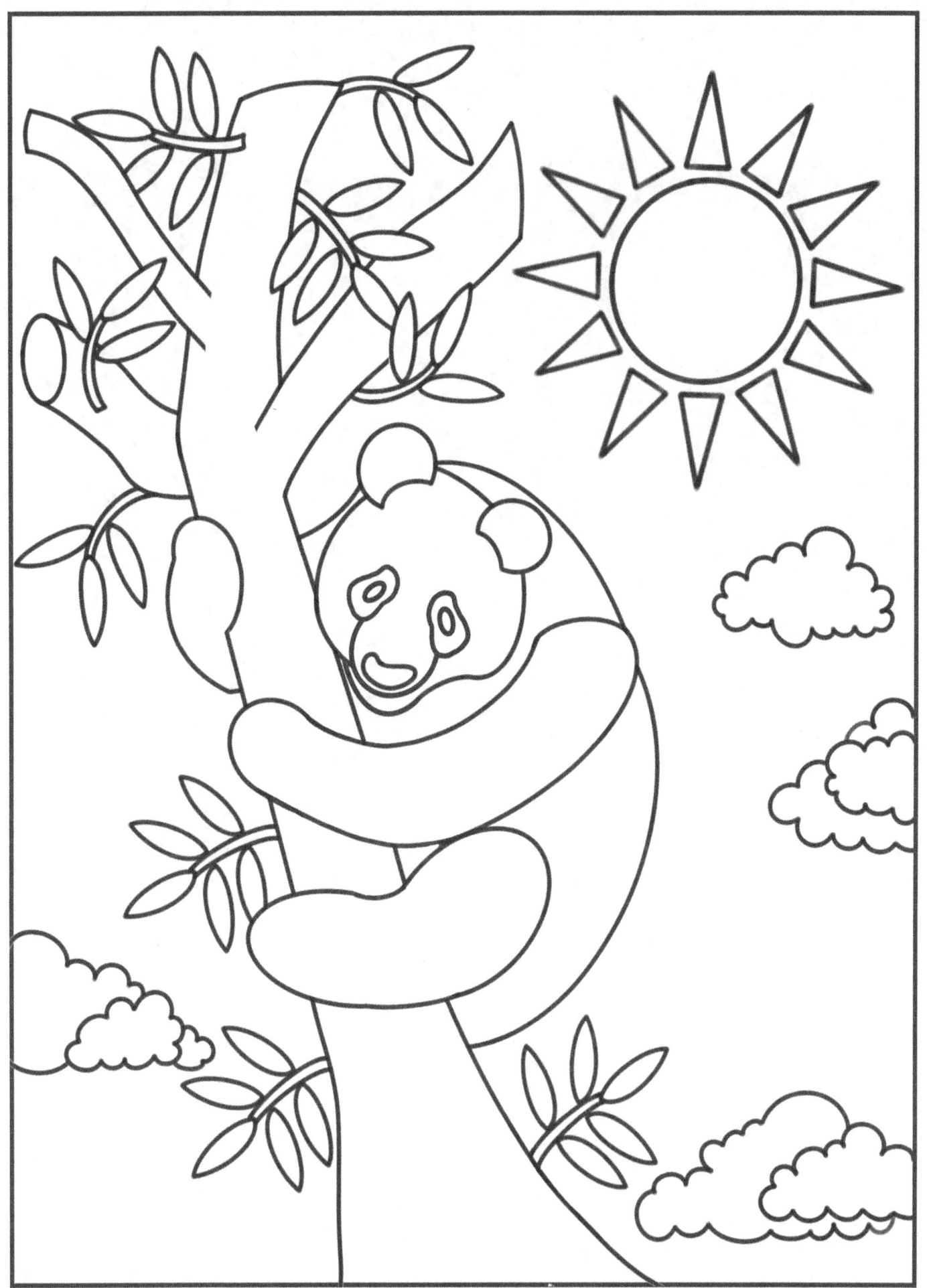

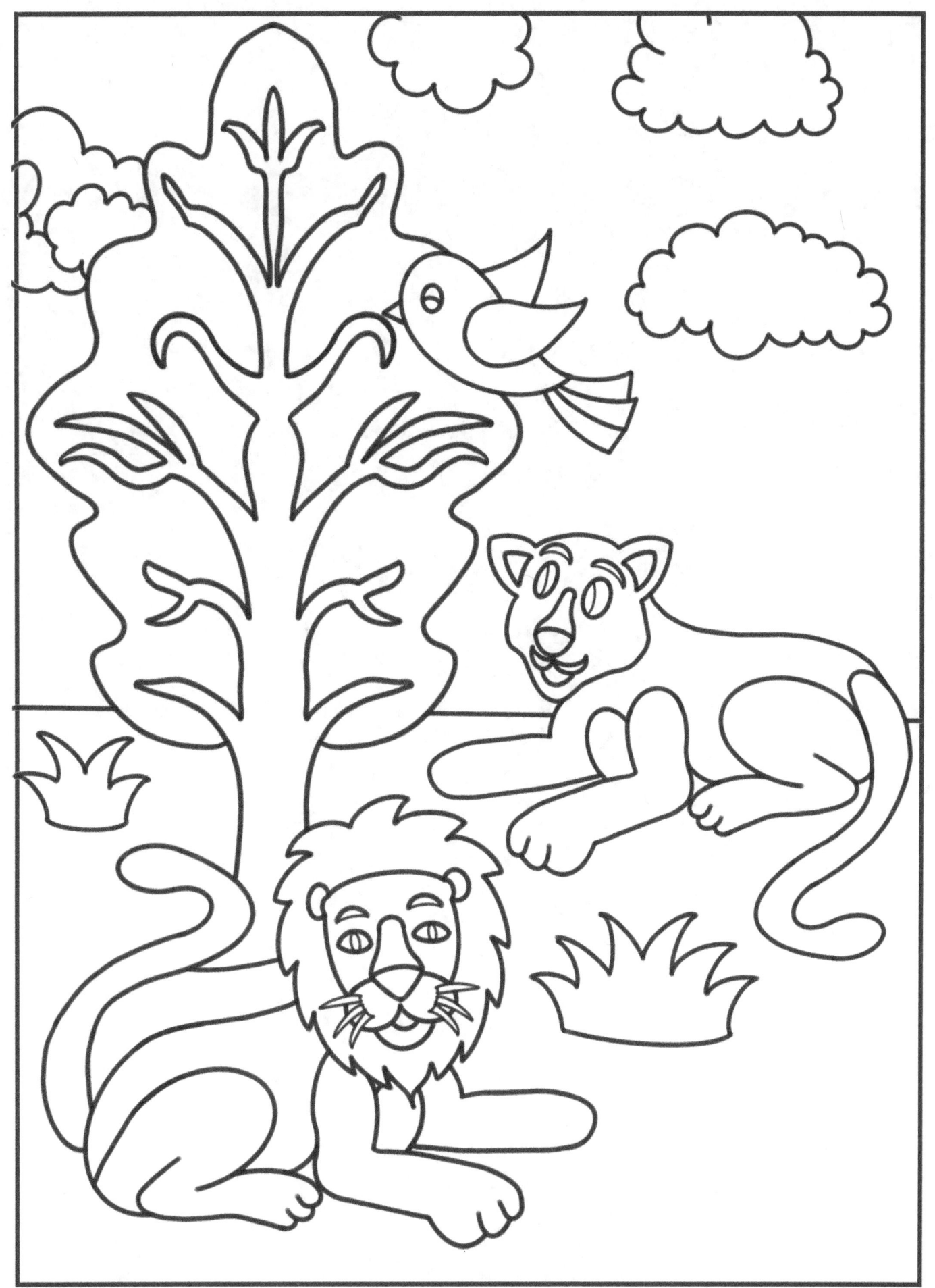

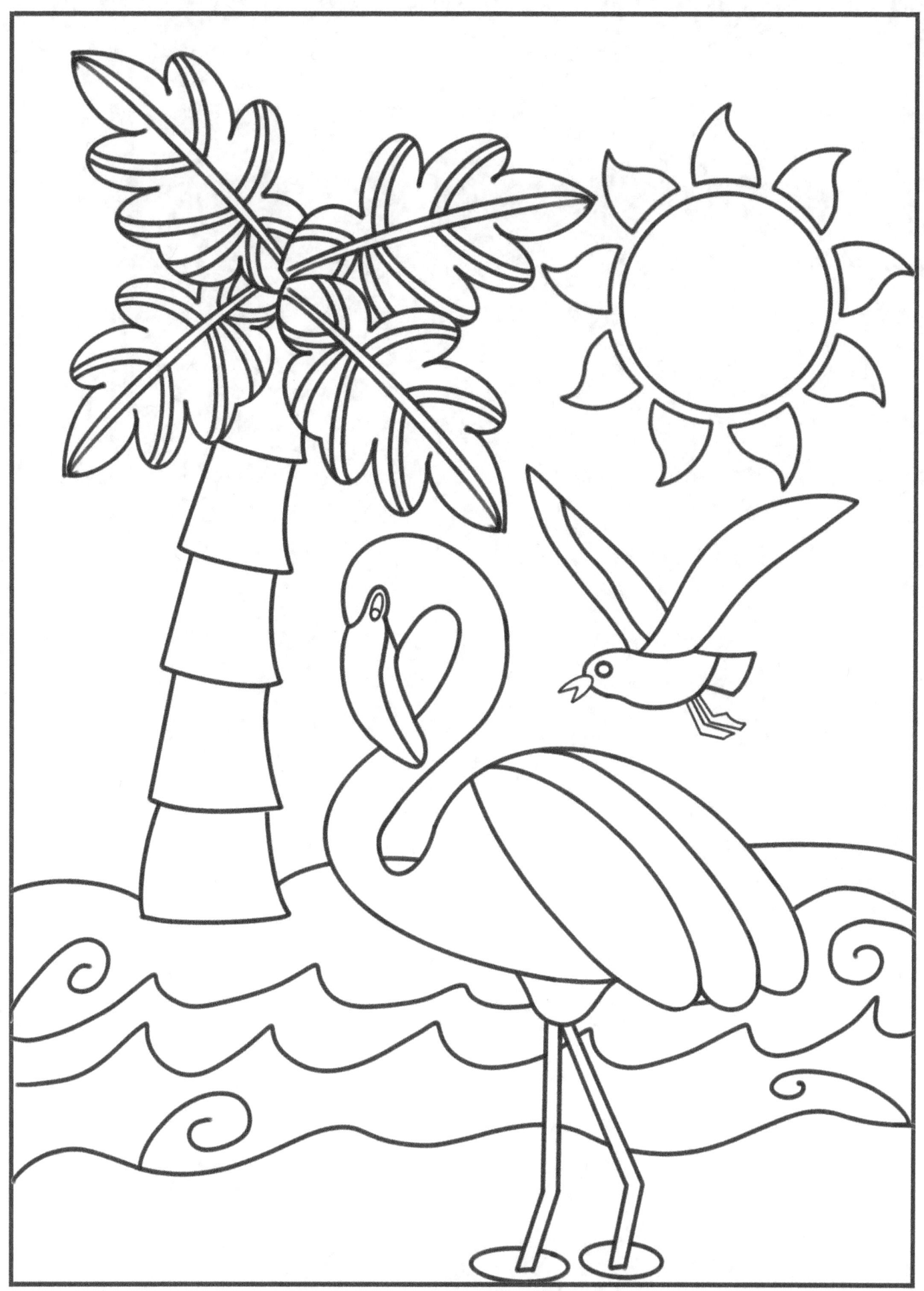

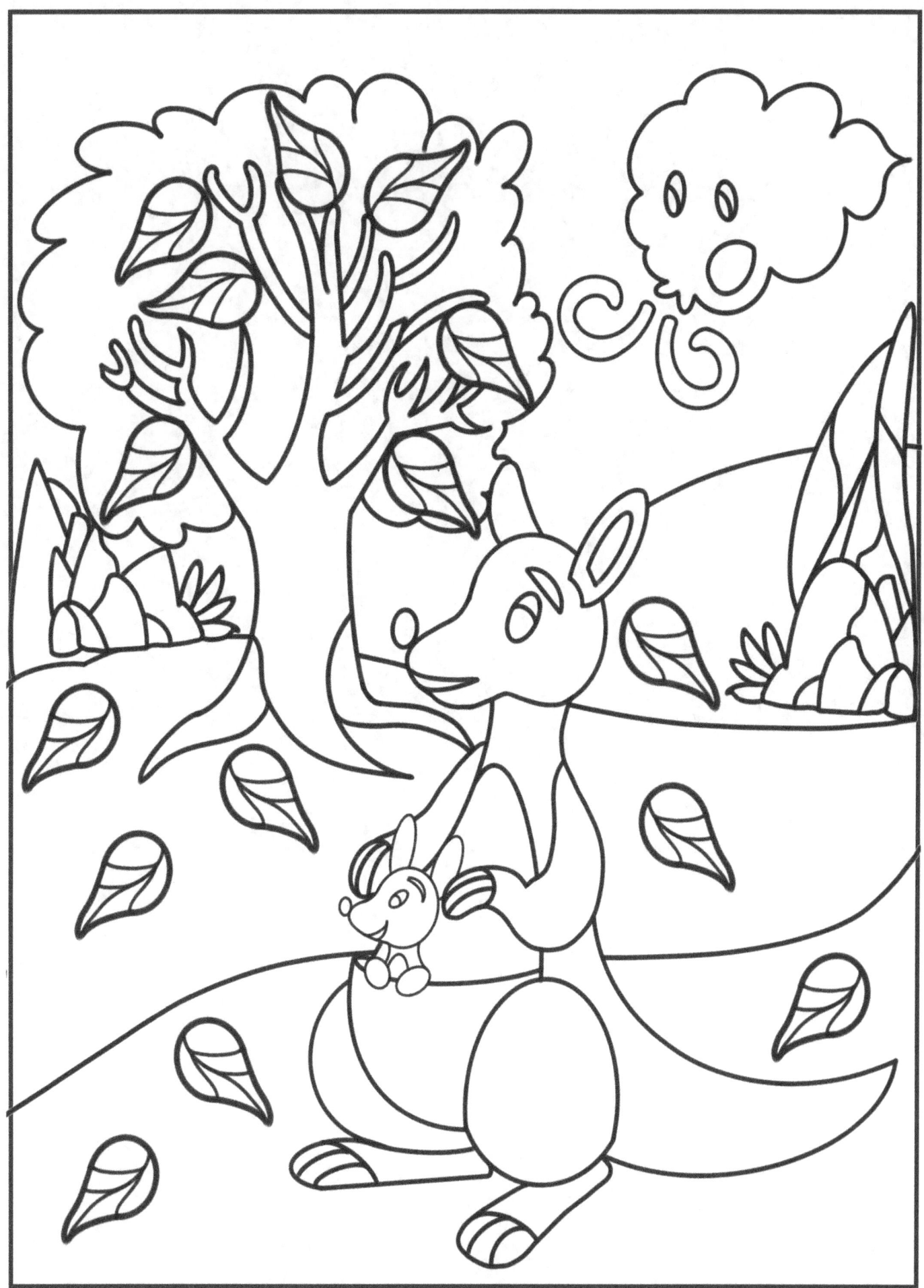

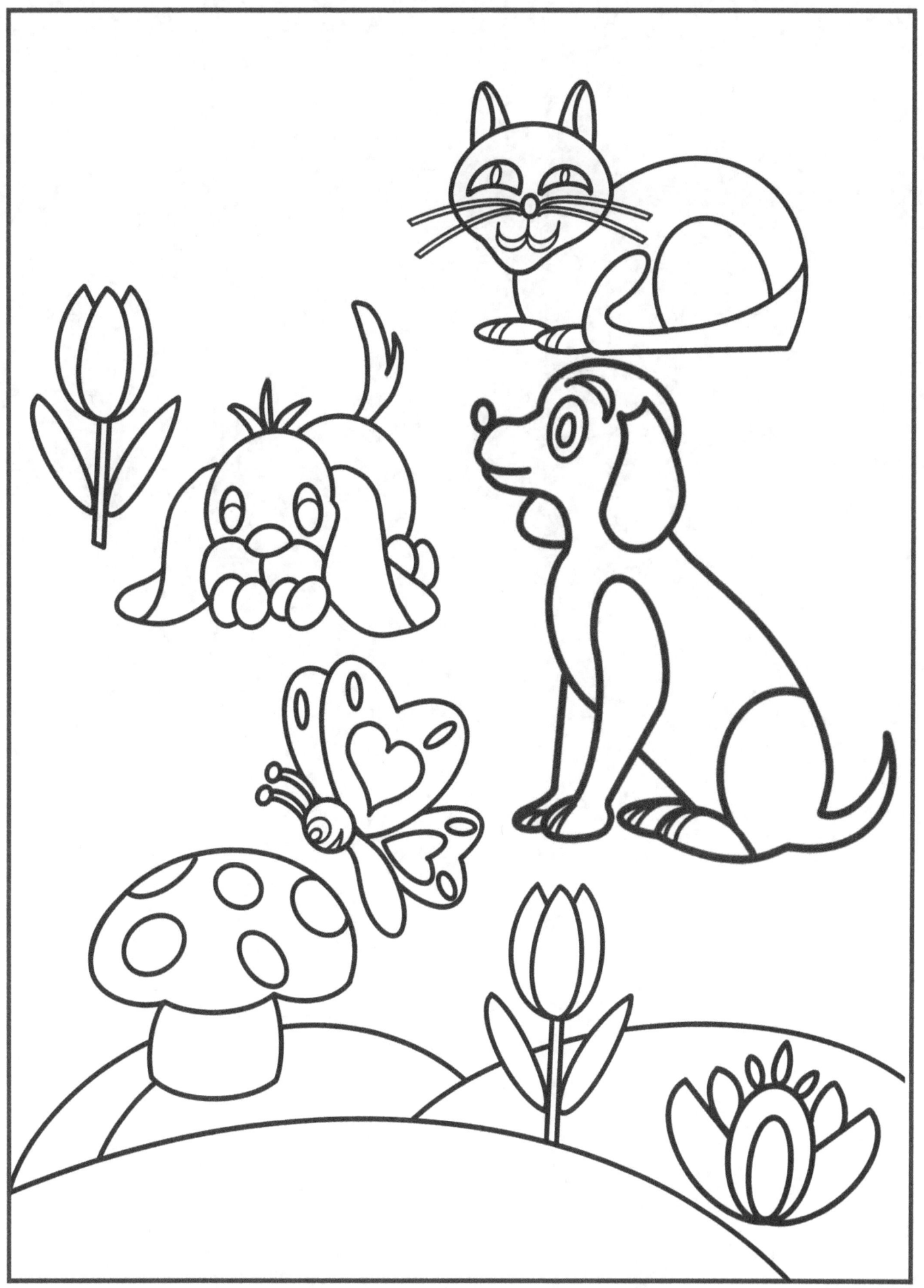

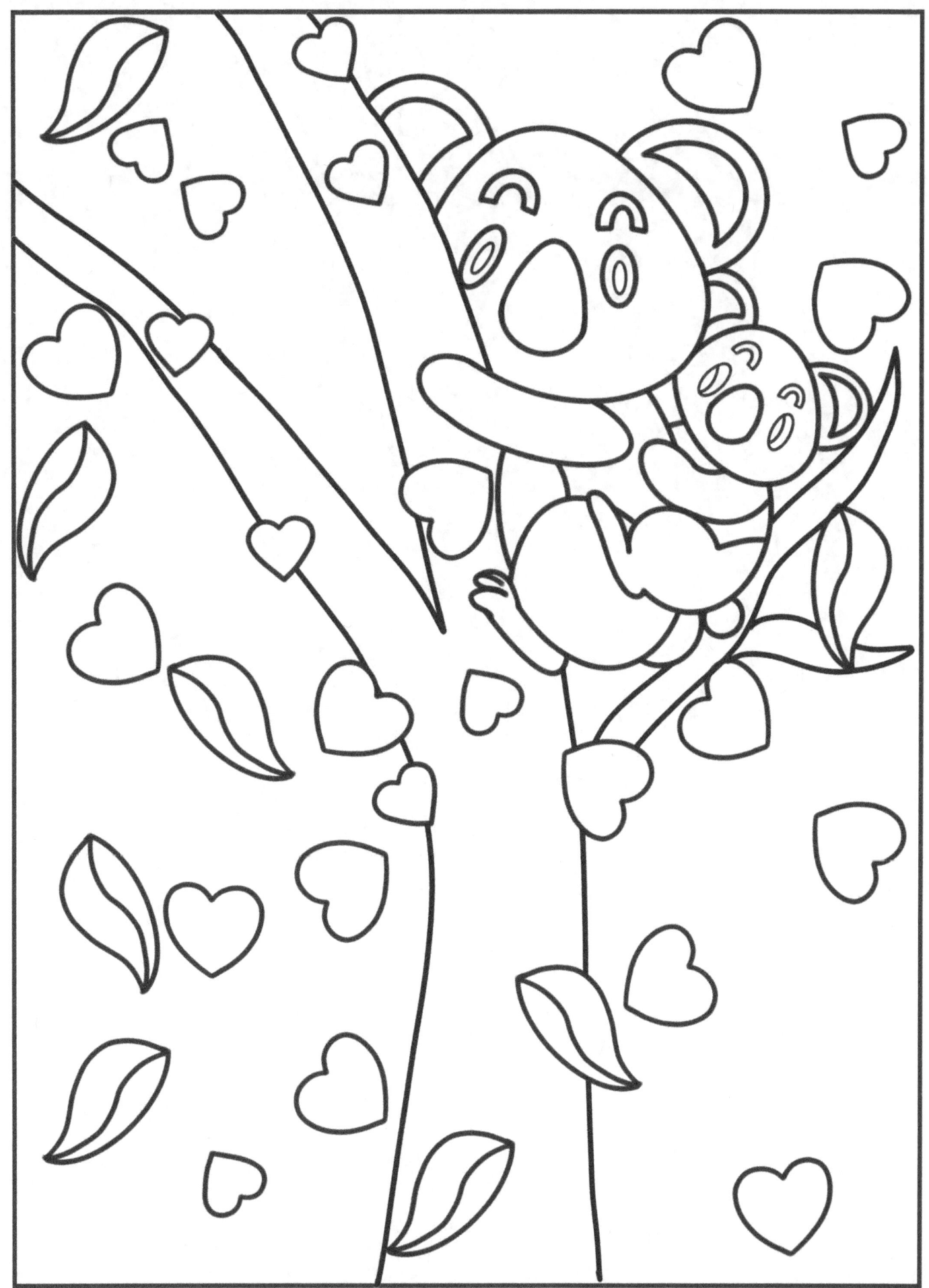

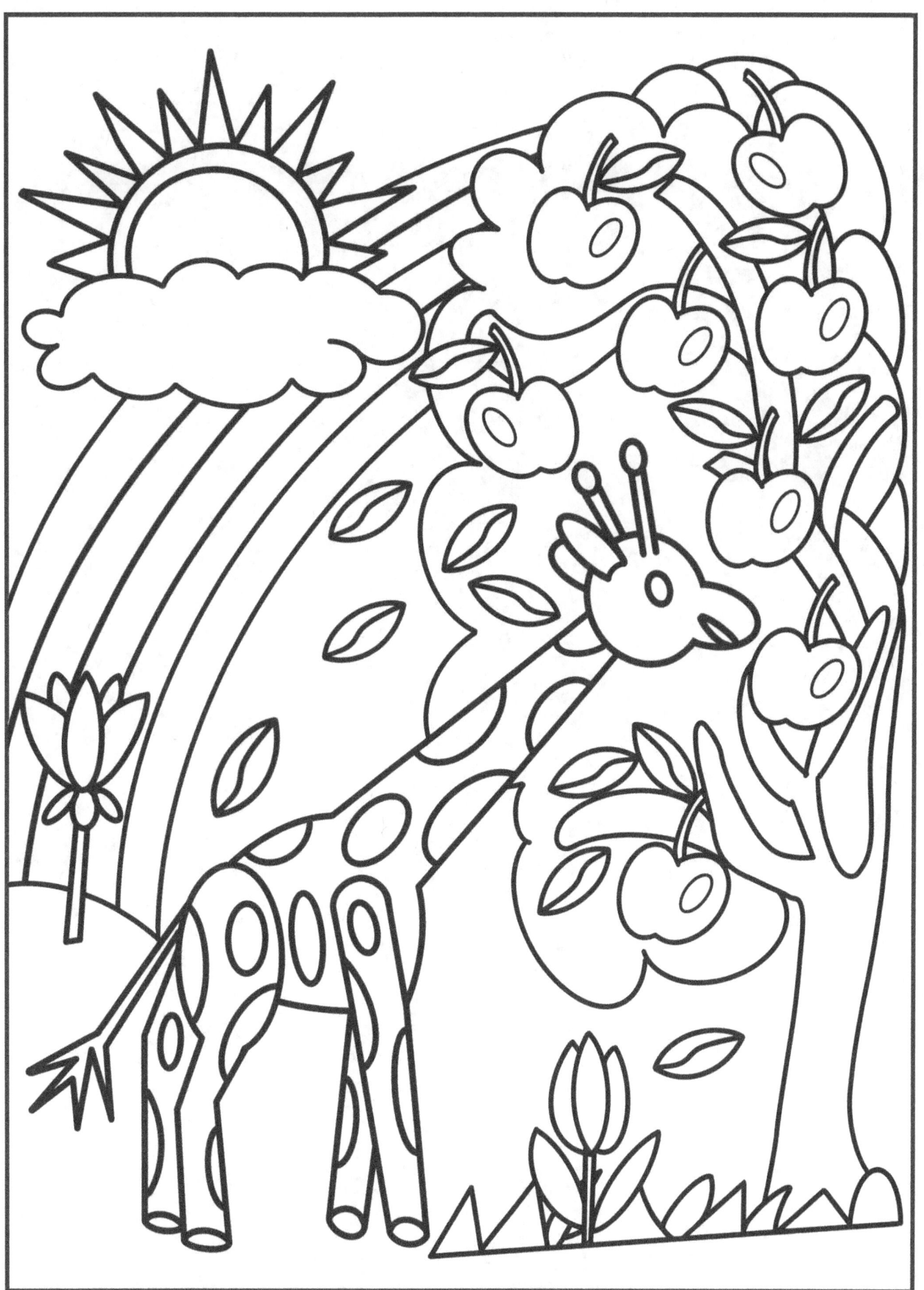

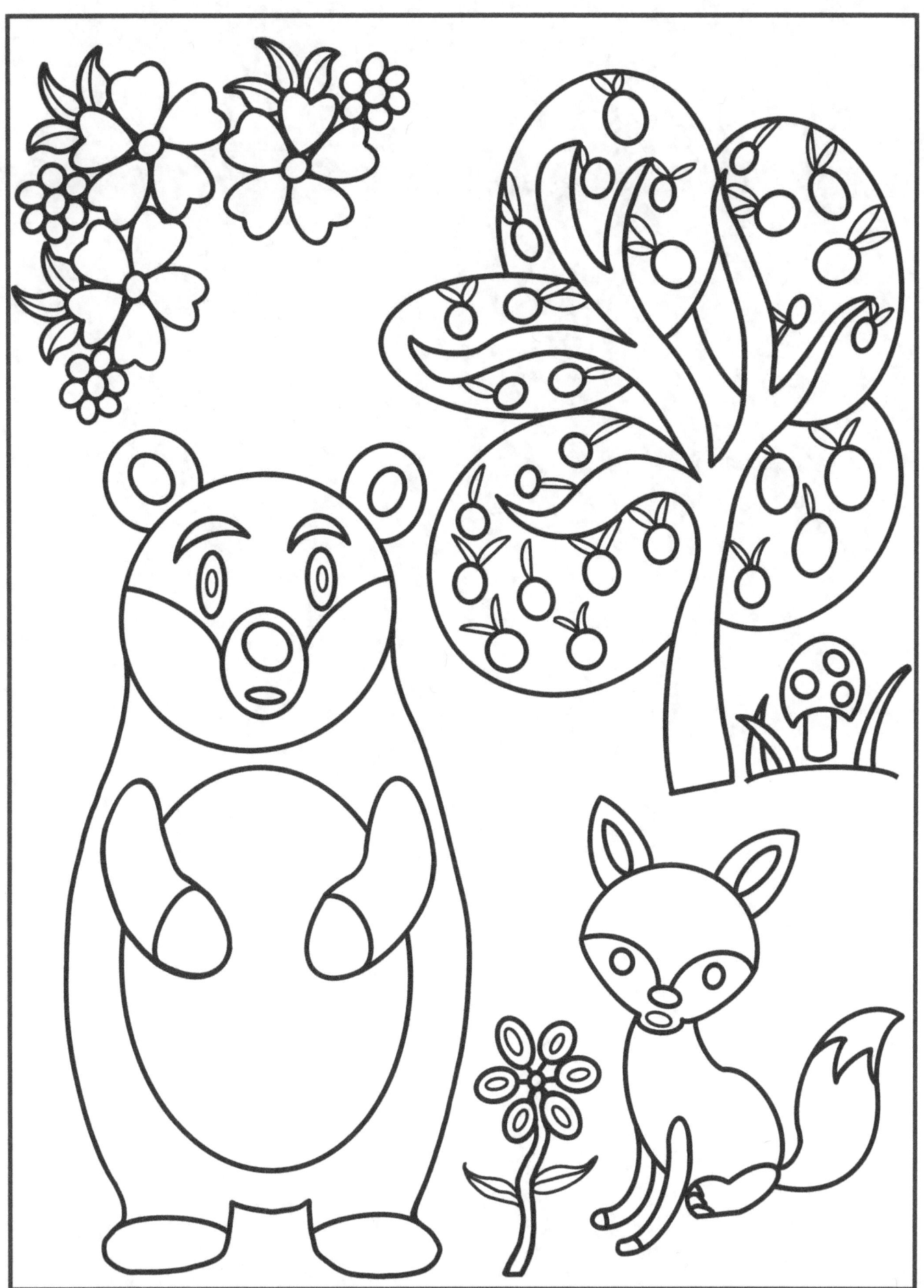

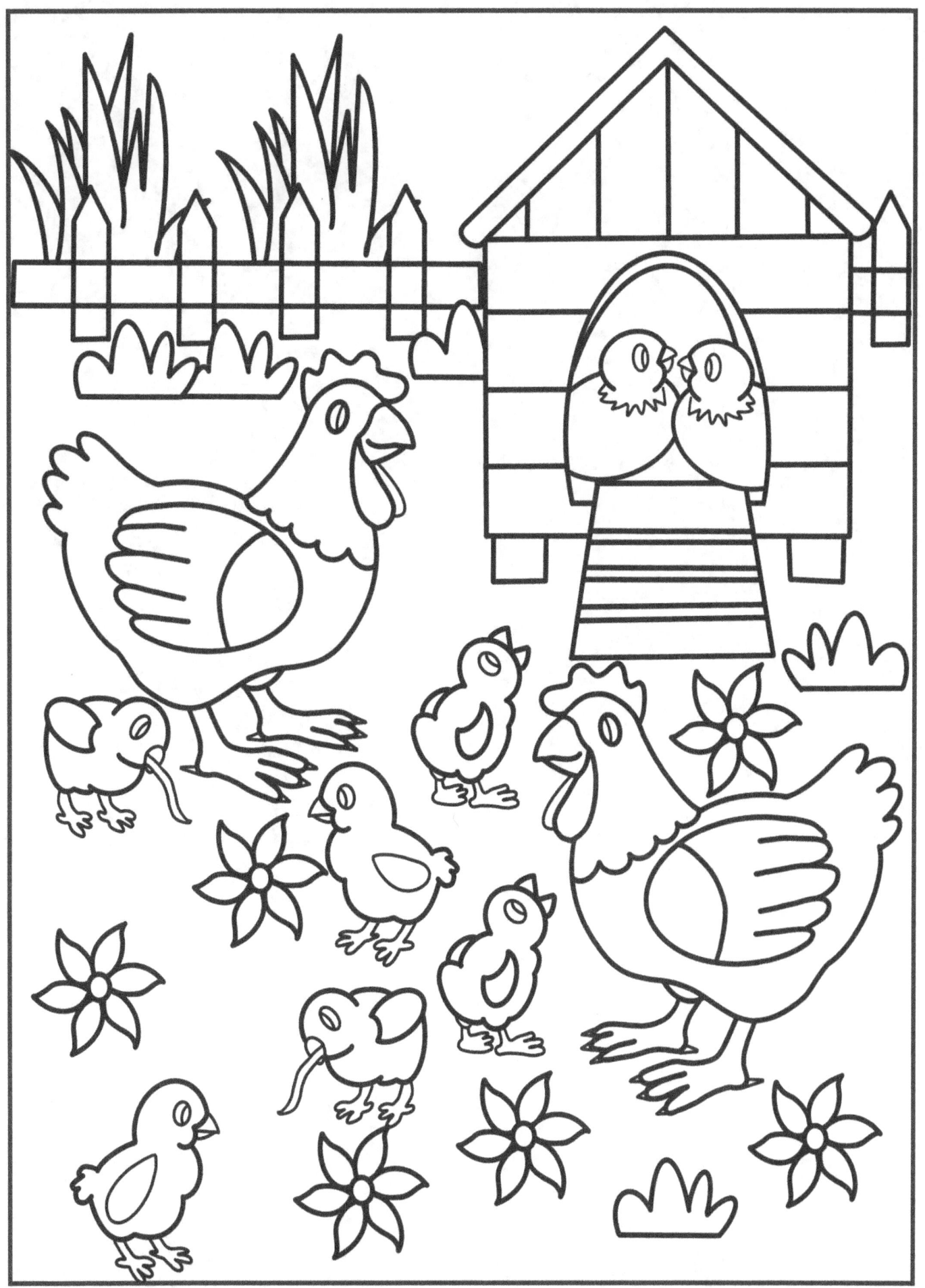

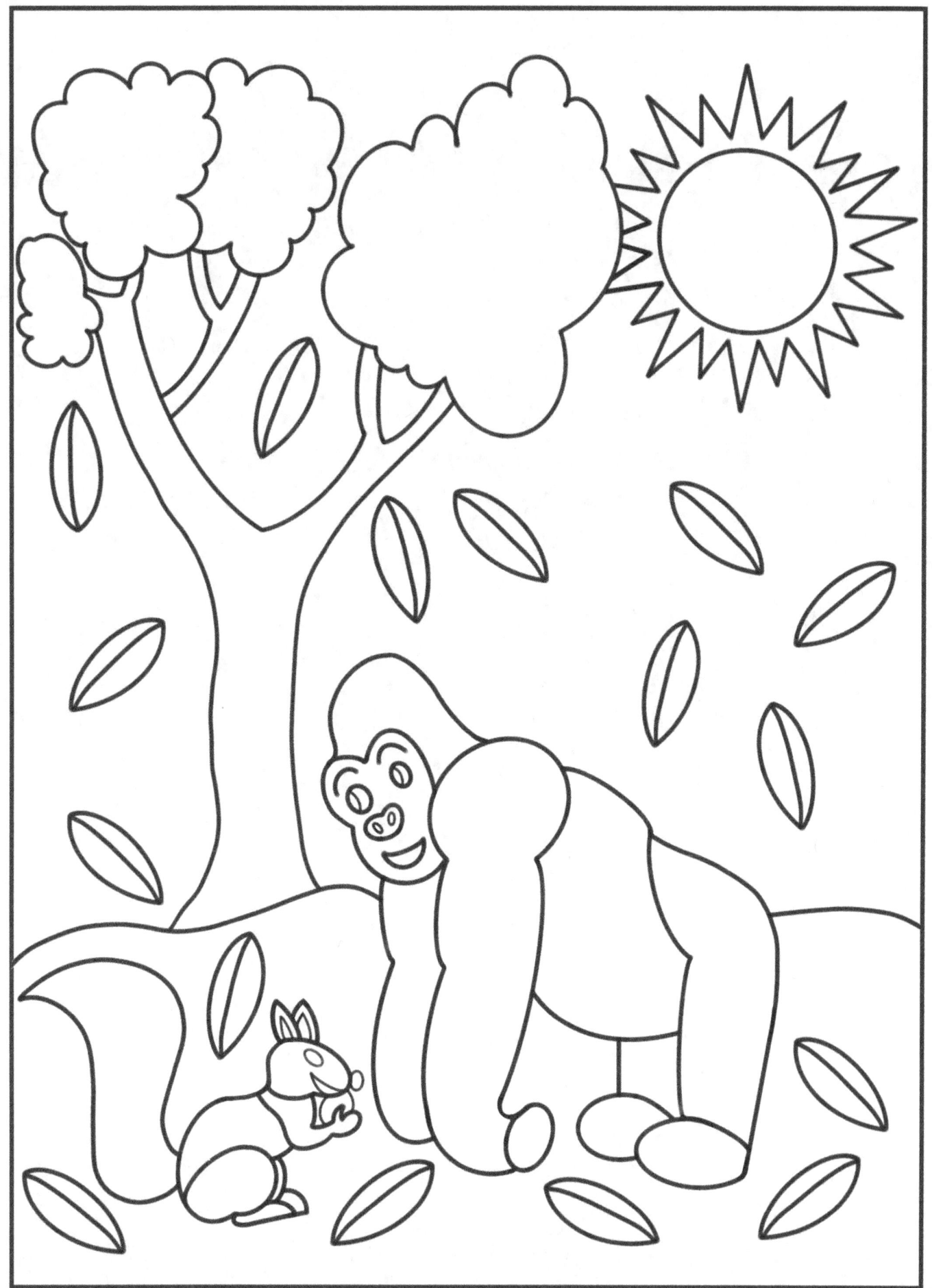

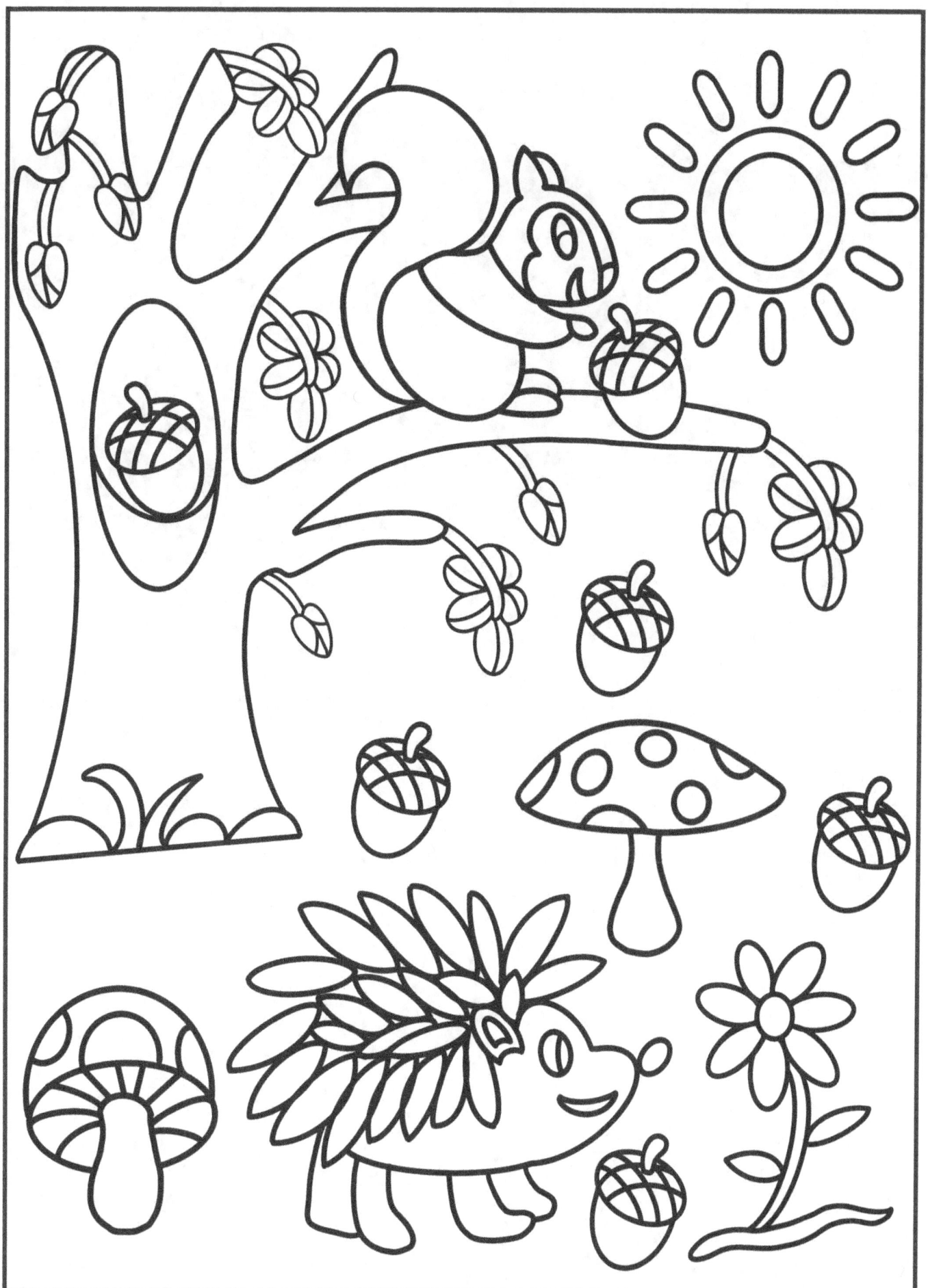

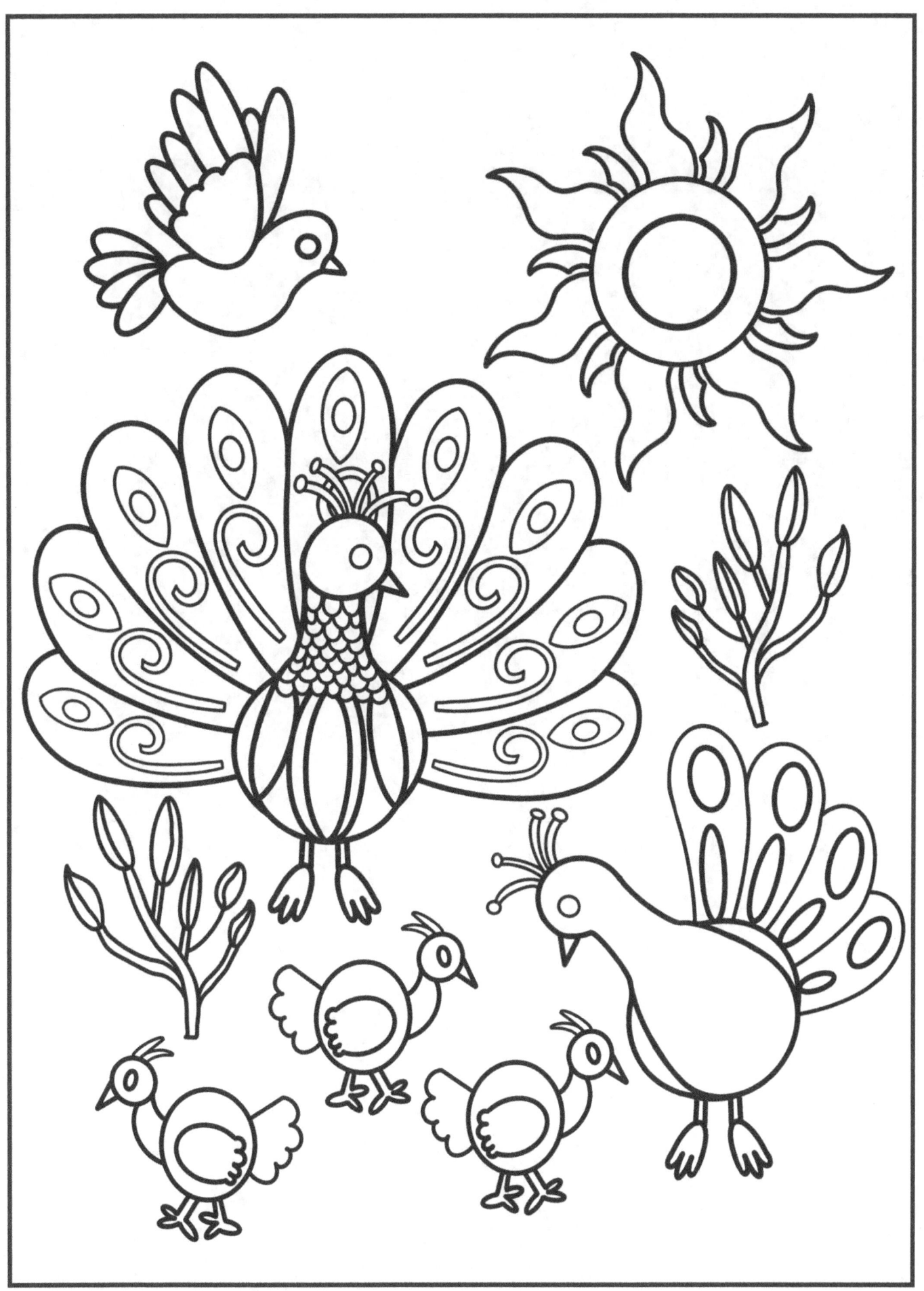

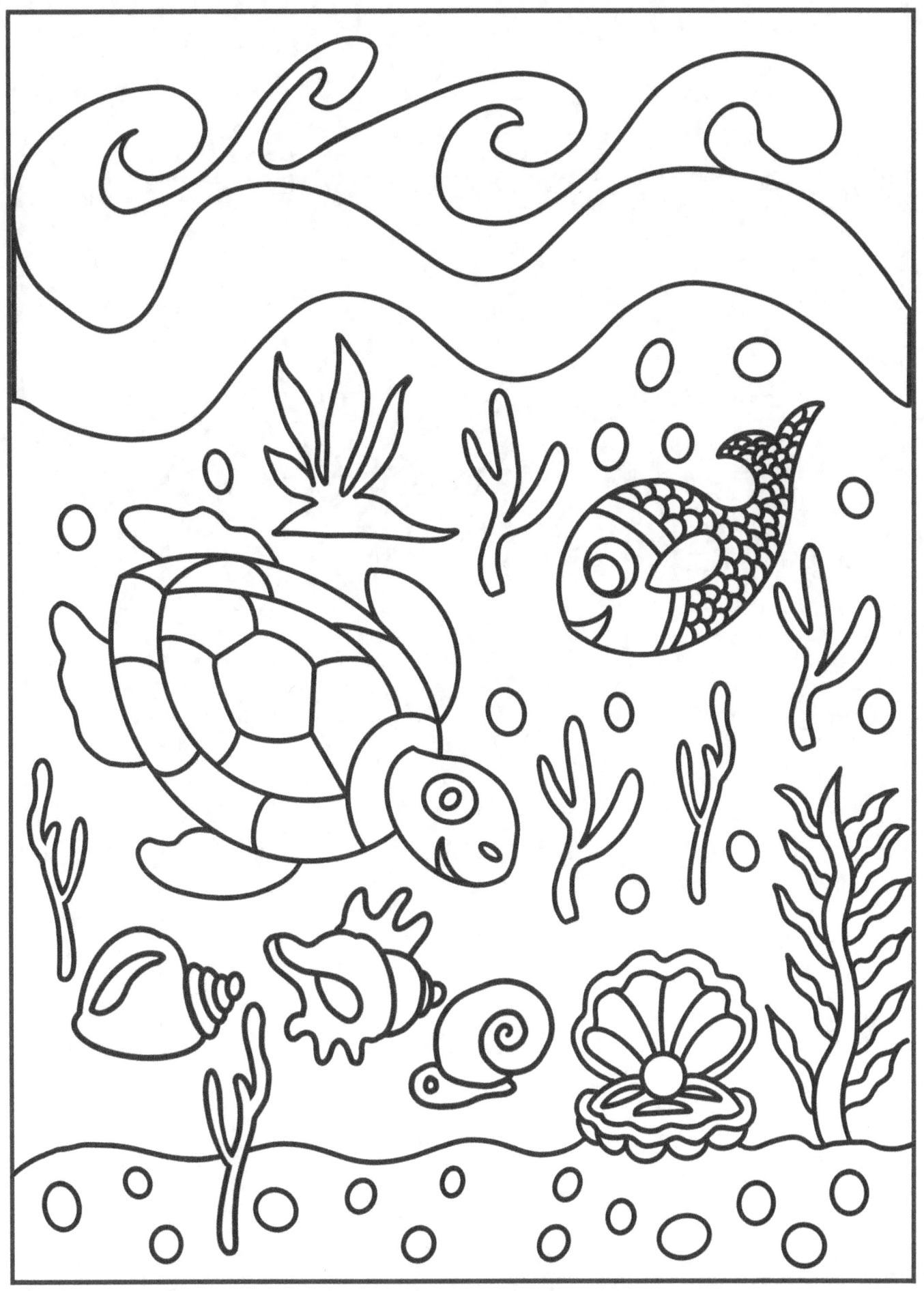

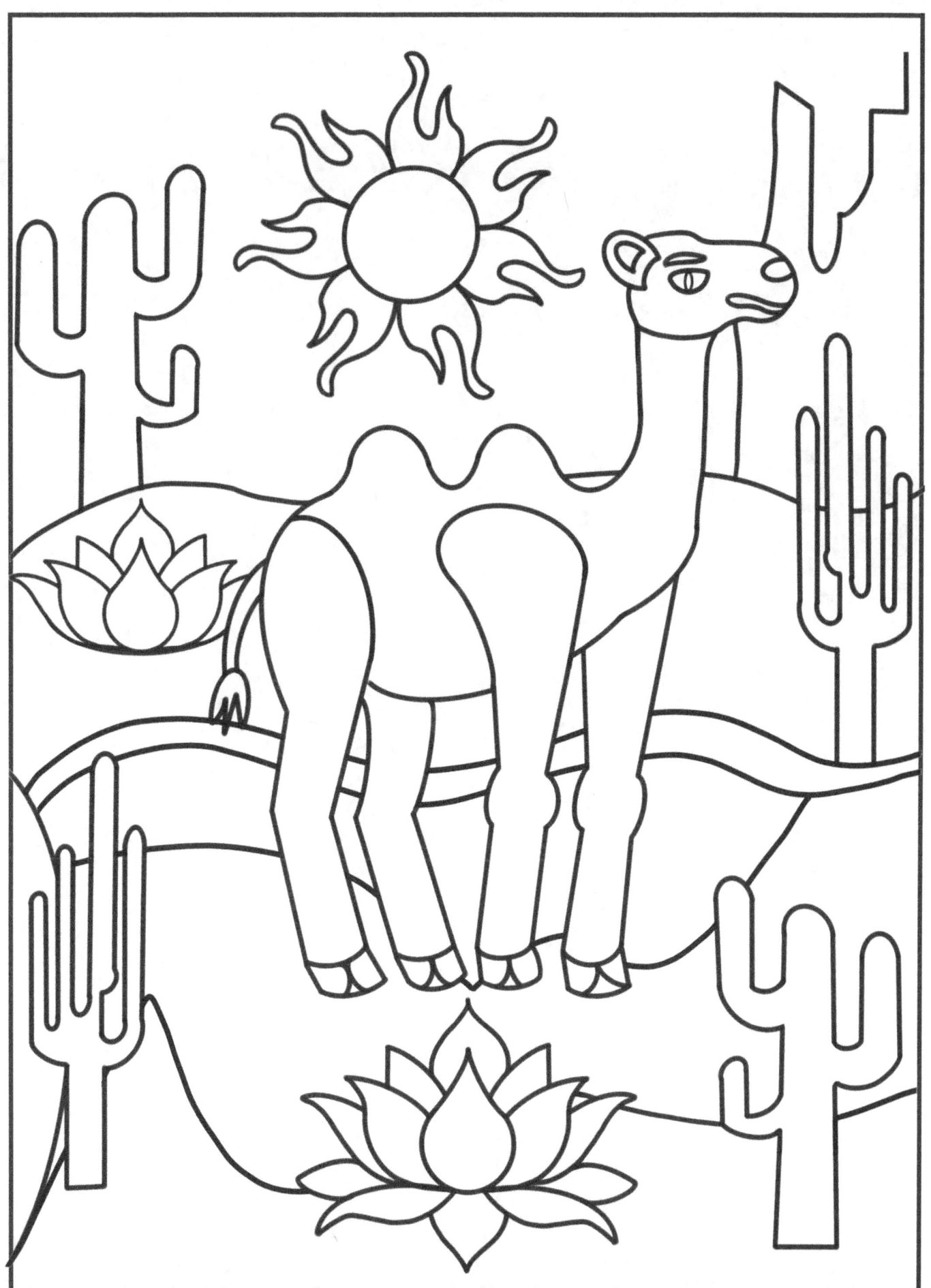

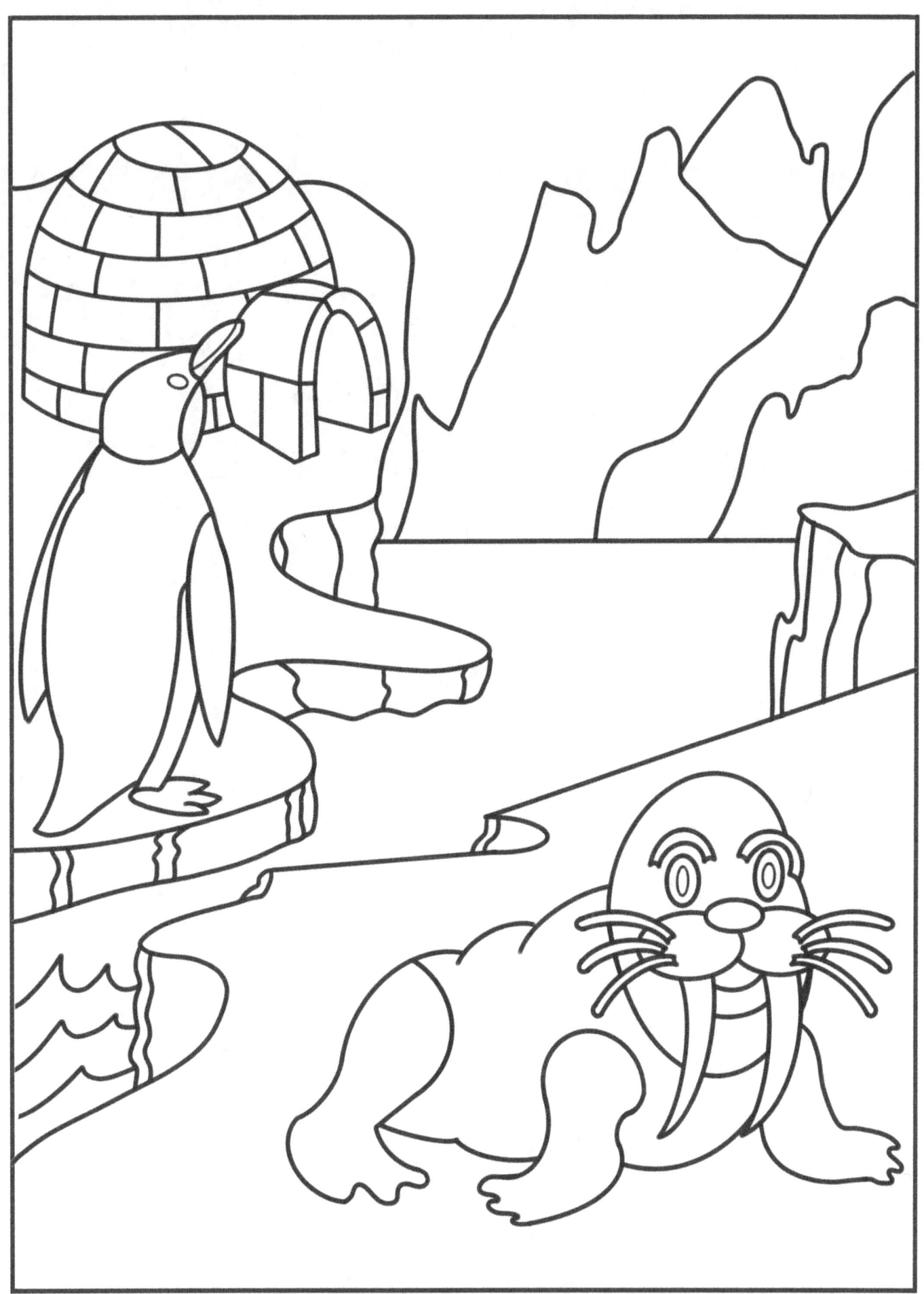

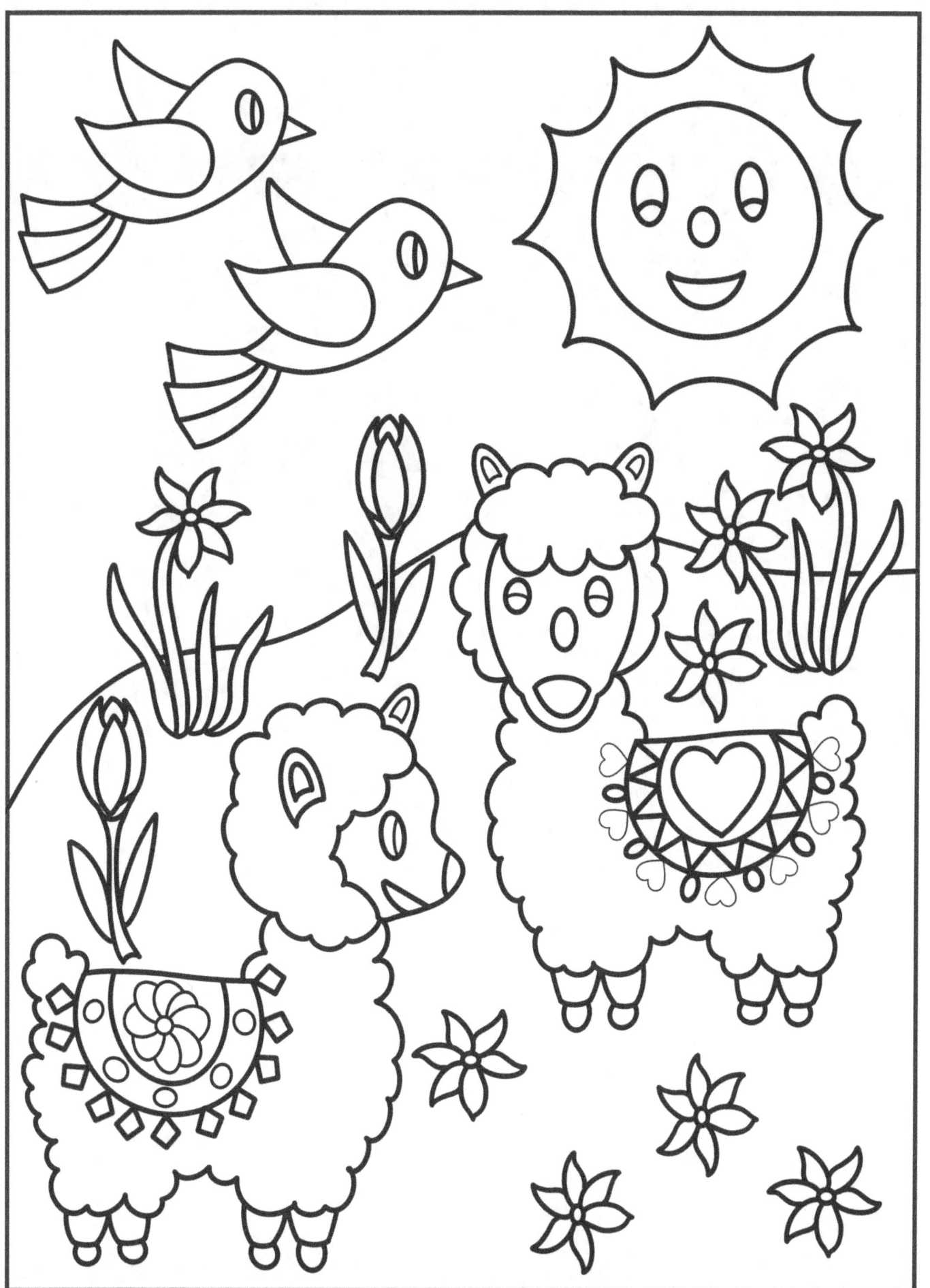

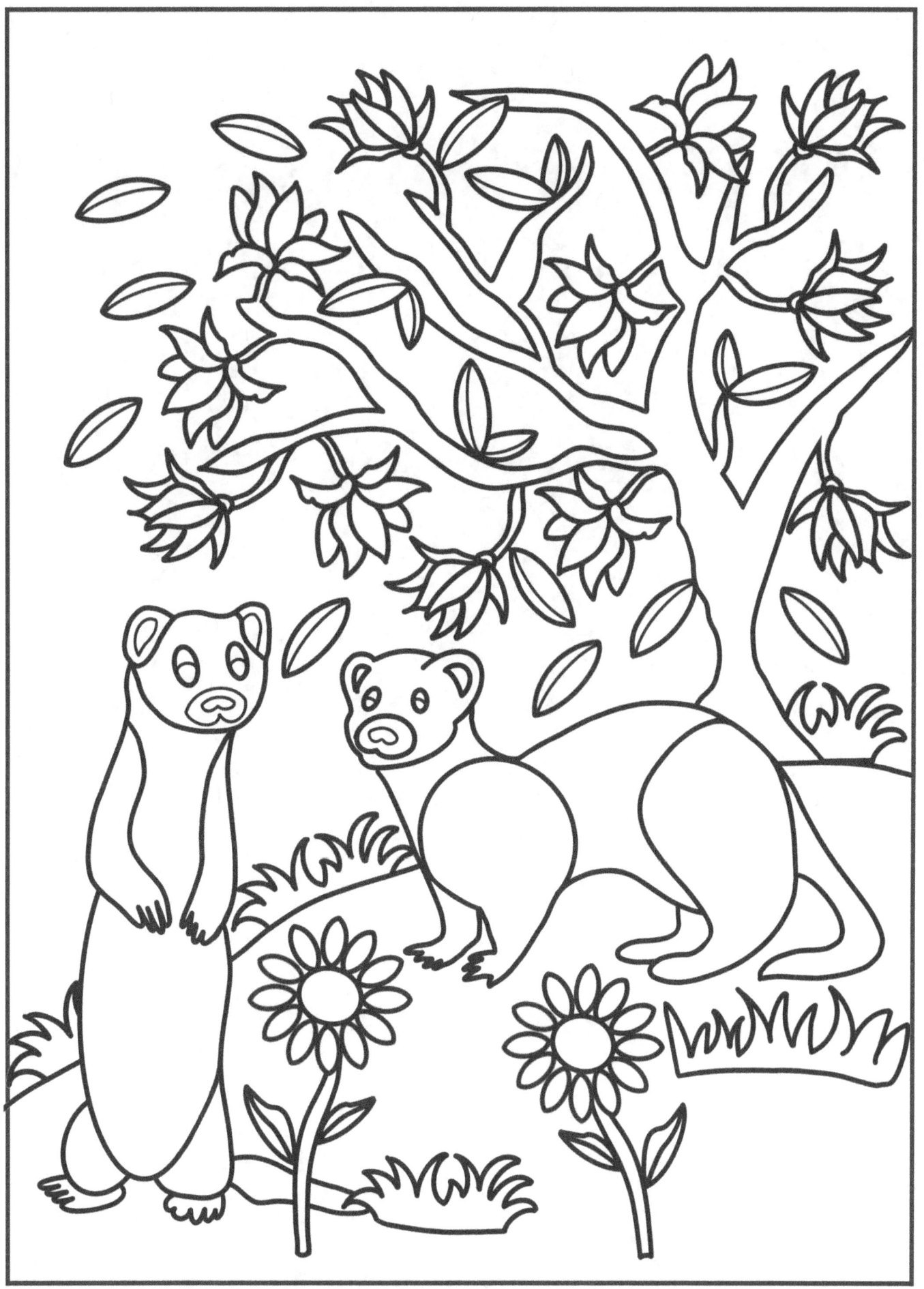

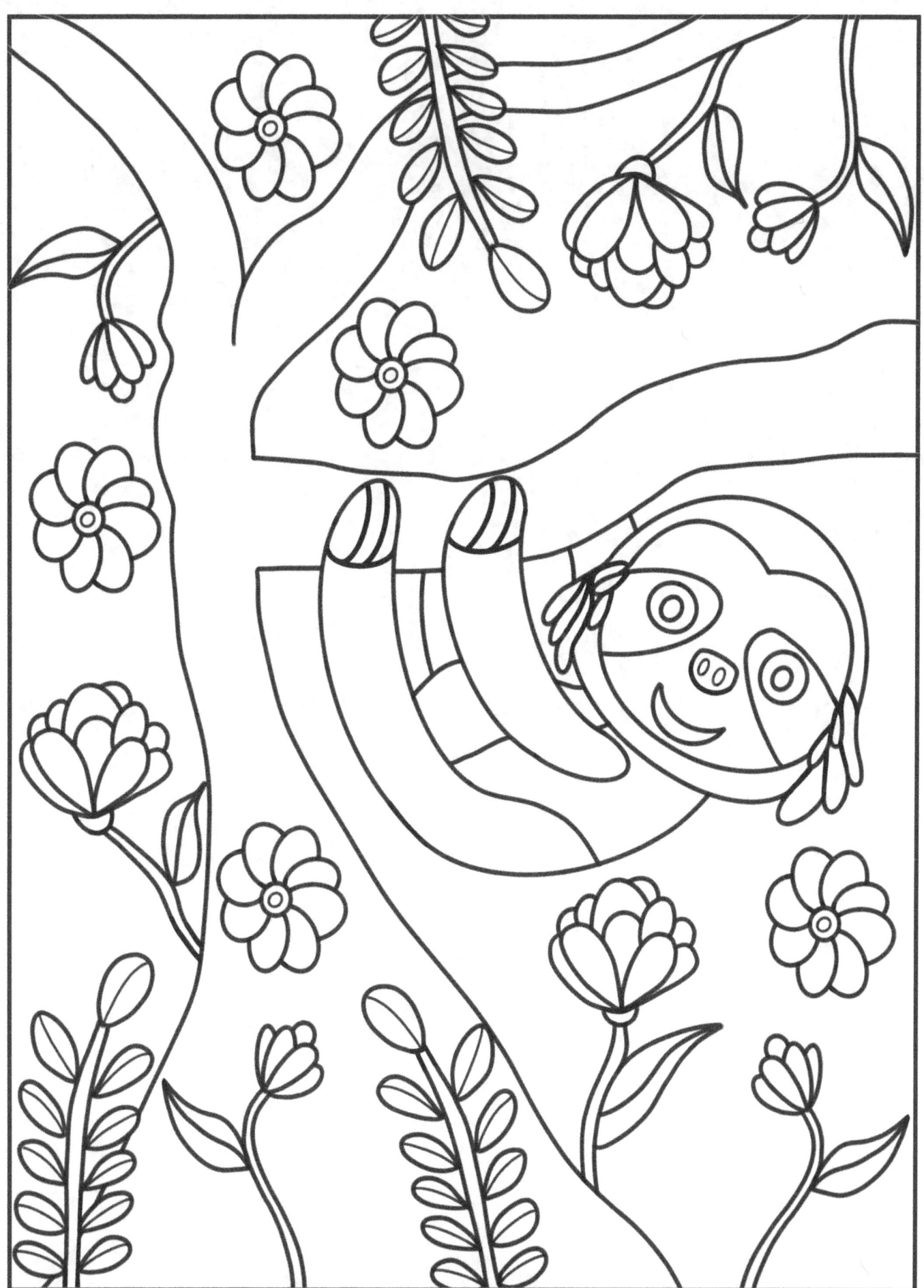

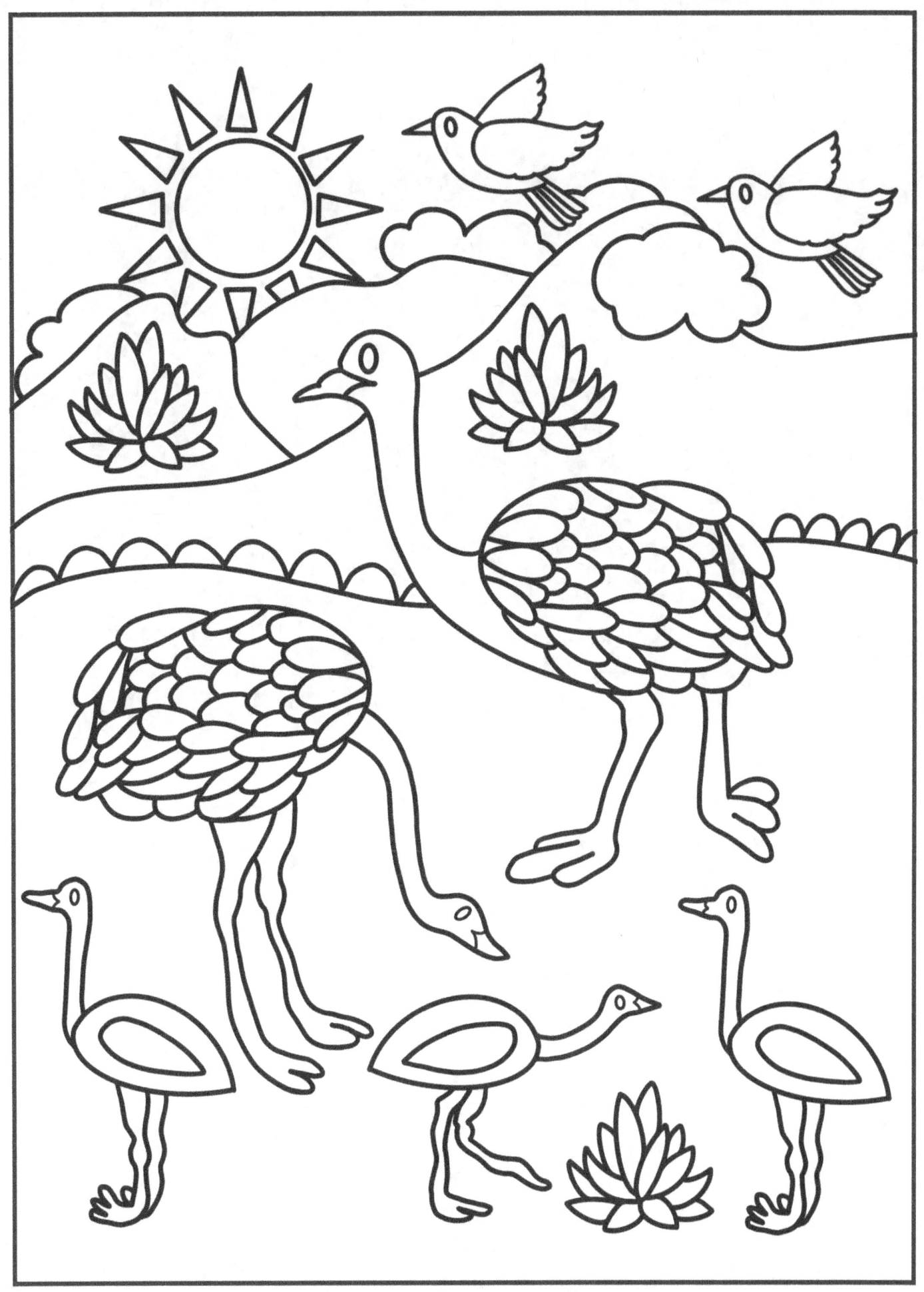

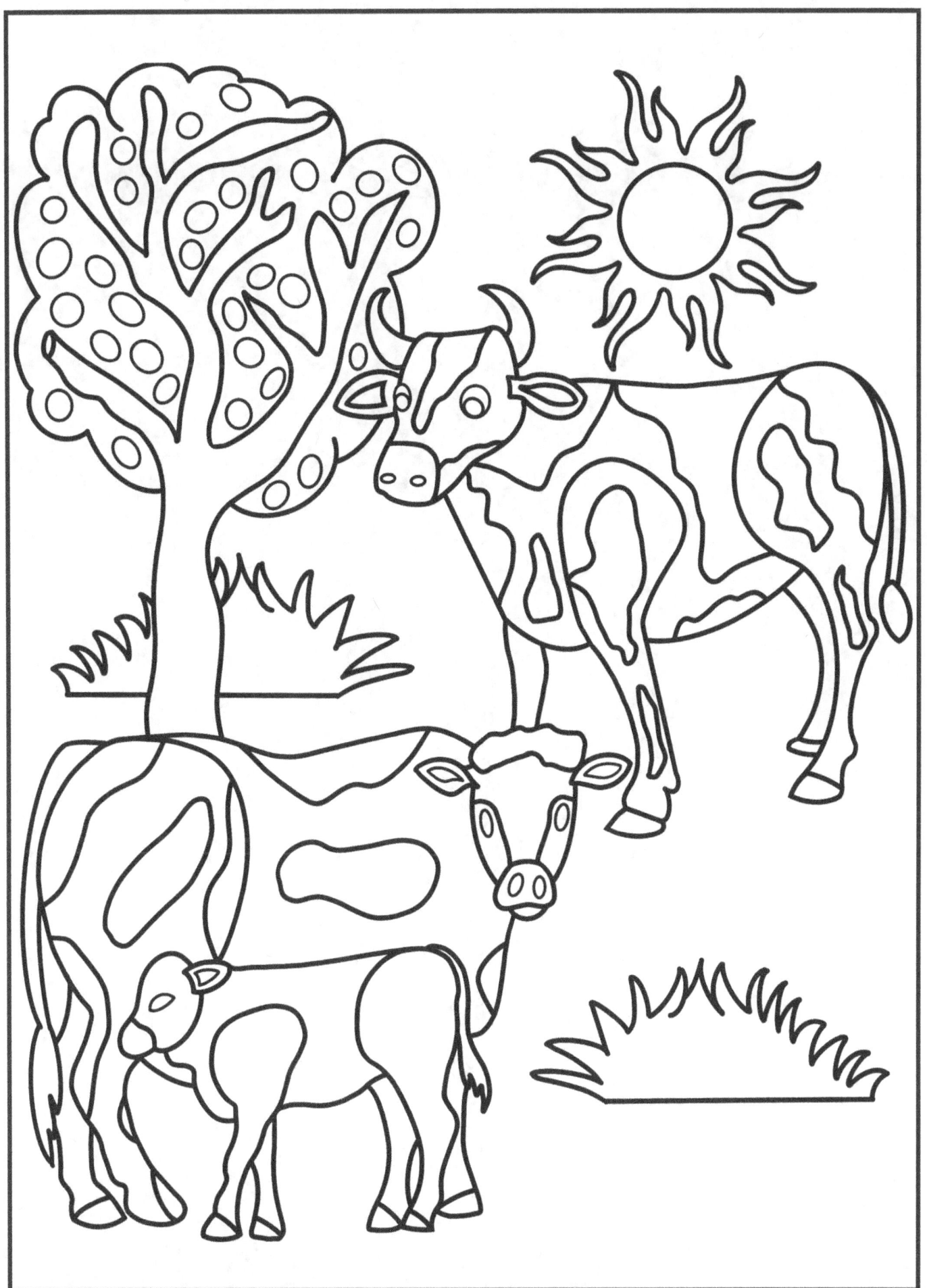

Hello there!

Thank you again for buying my book. It has been a great honor for me. Before you go, I need to ask you a big favor:

Would you be kind enough to review my book?

Your feedback allows me to improve the quality of my books and constantly come up with new, better ones.

Furthermore, reviews are the mechanism that makes a book visible and also what drives people to buy more. Probably you too read some reviews before buying this one.

So, if you enjoyed this book, I kindly ask you to please, take a few minutes of your time to post an honest review on Amazon.
I would really appreciate it.

With love,

Lupita

Cute Animals

Coloring Book for Children

This lovely coloring book for children includes a variety of happy and cute animals depicted in their natural habitat. Each illustration was developed by artist Lupita Romo keeping in mind pre-school and early school age children's coloring skills and it is designed to stimulate the child's creativity and imagination.

Coloring is a motor activity which stimulates children's brain development, improve their mood, help them relax, and tease their imagination. Your little artist will love coloring all the animals in this book. Just let your child embrace the beautiful and relaxing world of colors and anything can happen.

If you like this book, please take a moment to post a review on www.amazon.com

Enjoy.

Lupita Romo

About Lupita Romo

Lupita Romo grew up in a family of artists. Both her parents inspired her to appreciate art and to follow her passion which eventually led her to complete a Bachelor Degree in Graphic Design and a University Diploma in Art. She likes bright colours and simple forms and loves art seen through the eyes of children. She enjoys sharing her passion through teaching art and the theory of colors to children and seniors alike.

Cute Animals Coloring Book for Children

ISBN: 9798705299393

Other books you may enjoy by What A Colourful World :

Adult Coloring Books

Adult Coloring: Baby Animals
Adult Coloring Book: Animal Designs
Adult Coloring: Easy Animals (Black Background)
Adult Coloring: Easy Animals (White Background)
Adult Coloring Book: #Dadisms
Adult Coloring Book: #Momisms
Adult Coloring Book: Lovely Mandalas
Amazing Coloring
Amazing Coloring 2
Easy Coloring: Adult Coloring Book
Easy Designs: Large Print for Easy Coloring
Easy Flower Mandalas (Black Background)
Easy Flower Mandalas (White Background)
Easy Mandalas
Flowers for You!: Adult Coloring Book
Love Coloring Book
Mandalas for Beginners
Mandala Designs (Black Background)
Mandala Designs (White Background)
Simple Mandalas: An Adult Coloring Book
Sugar Skulls: Dia de los Muertos

Children Coloring Books

Cute Animals: Coloring Book for Children
Easy Coloring for Kids
Merry Christmas: Coloring Book for Children and Preschoolers
Tracing My First ABC

www.ingramcontent.com/pod-product-compliance
Lightning Source LLC
Chambersburg PA
CBHW081002220526
45467CB00008B/2659